From Tragedy to Triumph

Jeffrey Wills

Kingdom Publishing, LLC
1350 Blair Drive, Odenton, Maryland 21113
www.kingdompublishingllc.com
Printed in the United States of America

From Tragedy to Triumph

Copyright © 2018 by Jeffrey Wills

All rights reserved. No part of this book may be reproduced or transmitted in any form or by any means, electronic or mechanical, including photocopying, recording or by any information storage and retrieval system without written permission from the author, except for the inclusion of brief quotations in a review.

All scripture quotations are from the King James Version of the Bible. Thomas Nelson Publishers, Nashville: Thomas Nelson, Inc. 1972.

Editor: Kimberly Curtis

Typist: Cartia Brown-Morgan
        Tech-Ayd

LCCN: 2018943174

ISBN 978-1-947741-12-6

Acknowledgments

I want to especially thank our pastors for their prayers, love, support, spiritual guidance through the darkest times of our lives. Janice and I truly appreciate their ability to walk with where we were on our path through this struggle and assist us with our journey through it all. I also want to thank my Pastors who encouraged me to write my story.

Pastor Aaron Jones and Pastor (First Lady) Sharon Jones of New Hope Church of God, Waldorf, Maryland

Pastor Bobby Holmes and First Lady Melody Holmes of Deliverance Church of Christ, Capitol Heights, Maryland.

Lastly, special thanks go to those friends and family members for their assistance in proofreading and editing these chapters. I know this is just the beginning.

Table of Contents

Introduction It Was Just A Normal Day

    How My Wife and I Met 1

Chapter 1 The Beginning of the End 5

Chapter 2 Our Story – The Day of Darkness 9

Chapter 3 Many Months After 17

Chapter 4 Relationship with My Son 21

Chapter 5 You Never Know 25

Chapter 6 Our Lives Today 29

Message to the Parents 35

*All names have been changed except for those of the family – Shea Proctor, Janice Proctor and Jeffrey Wills. In addition, Jeffrey's place of employment has been changed.

FROM TRAGEDY TO TRIUMPH

~~~~~~

"Nay, in all these things we are more than conquerors through him that loved us."

Romans 8:37

Introduction

"It Was Just a Normal Day"
How My Wife and I Met

I was twenty-two years old when I told my mother that I was moving out. Despite her disagreement, I had decided that I needed to begin living for myself. A friend of mine, Derek Duarte had called me and said he was going to visit his girlfriend at her house. Derek asked if I wanted to go with him. He said she had sisters that were very attractive. I declined. Two hours later, Derek and a few of our friends came down to my mother's house. We all had low rider trucks. He asked me again to go with him to his girlfriend's house; this time I agreed to go.

It seemed that GOD had touched my heart to go with him, but I did not know it was Him at the time. I did not know HIS plan was to introduce me to a very kind and beautiful young woman. Her name was Janice Proctor. When I saw Janice, she was walking with another man, but I knew that she was the one for me. I had already claimed that one day she would be my wife. I thank GOD that I listened to my heart. I continued to visit every day, but she didn't know I was coming to see her. On July 19, 1988, Janice's sister told her that I was outside. Janice became curious and asked, "Who is this young man?" as she came out to see me.

Unbeknownst to Janice, the man that was walking with her on the first day I came to her sister's house, was married. After she found out, she cut ties with him and we began dating. I met her son, Shea Proctor, who was eight years old at the time. I really liked Shea, and we began spending a lot of time together. I would take Shea to his best friend's house quite often. We played basketball with his friends and played football games. He enjoyed going for rides and just talking.

One day I knelt and asked Janice to give me a chance in a relationship with her. She told me that I was too young, but I was determined to have her as my girlfriend. I begged her again, and she finally agreed. Shea began looking to me as a good friend. He did not know his father, so I took on the role of a father-figure in his life. I believed I needed to be there for him in all ways, love, discipline and to be the role model that had been absent in his life.

Janice and I married on December 13, 1992 at Deliverance Church of Christ, Capitol Heights, Maryland. Shea was fourteen years old at the time.

Page left blank intentionally

FROM TRAGEDY

TO

TRIUMPH

~~~~~~

"And he said, Hearken ye, all Judah, and ye inhabitants of Jerusalem, and thou king Jehoshaphat, Thus saith the LORD unto you, Be not afraid nor dismayed by reason of this great multitude; for the battle is not yours, but God's."

2 Chronicles 20:15

Chapter 1

The Beginning of the End

Janice, Shea, and I moved to a town house in Laurel, Maryland after we got married. We lived there for six years. Shea began hanging with his friends and getting into trouble with the police. He was about fourteen years old, underage and selling drugs.

On one quiet evening, I was looking out the window and saw Shea beating up a man who was trying to buy drugs. I ran outside to stop him as I could see that the man was bleeding badly. I took the man inside of my house and put bandages on his face as I yelled at Shea and asked, "What is wrong with you?"

Several years later, I took a job at a crab house named Roger's Crab House. The managers' names were Roger and Brenda. I worked there for about six years, during which time Brenda informed me she had a house for rent. Janice and I looked at the house and decided to buy it. Janice, Shea and I moved again. On several occasions, I found Shea sleeping in the driveway because of his alcohol and drug problem. I tried to help him, but he seemed to be getting worse.

Shea had taken a few jobs working in restaurants, but they never lasted very long. As time passed, I decided to buy him a car. He began spending more time with friends, drinking excessively, and getting into trouble with police again; so much so that he was arrested. Shea was about fifteen years old, so he was sent to Boy's Village for about two years. Janice and I would visit him occasionally and try to encourage him to stay out of trouble. When he finally came home, I told Shea he needed to get his life together and stop getting arrested. Unfortunately, it wasn't long before Shea would find himself in more trouble.

Shea got in trouble again, and this time was sent to Old Dominion Camp for Boys because he was about seventeen. He spent about two years there. Janice and I visited him now and then, but it was a two-and-a-half-hour trip from where we lived. We would talk to him about plans for his future once he was released to come home. The first step in his plan was to get a job. One year later, after Shea's release, he totaled his car because he was driving under the influence of alcohol. It was amazing that he did not die in the accident. Surprisingly, he still did not learn his lesson and Shea's behavior was getting worse. Janice and I sat down with him and discussed his actions and decision making. I told him that we could no longer tolerate what he was doing with his life. We told him that if there was no change in his lifestyle, he would no longer be allowed to live at home. After that discussion, Shea started doing well. He would do good for a while but would eventually relapse. Janice and I told Shea it was time for him to grow up and move out.

Shea would come to see me at my job, Mover's Truck Leasing to ask about moving back in with us. I eventually found Shea sleeping in his car in the Mover's parking lot. He told me that he did not have anywhere to live so I felt sorry for him and told him to talk to his mother. Janice and I spoke about allowing Shea to move back in with us and we both agreed to it. We told him, he needed to get serious and stop getting into trouble. Shea did good for about two years.

One day I was helping my sister's friend, Tamra move and after the move I met Shea's half-brother. We had been talking and concluded that he was related to Shea. I went home and told Shea that I met his half-brother. I later introduced them to each other and they began hanging out. Shea started drinking again.

Shea began dating a girl named Aurora and they dated for a while before ending their relationship. After their break-up, Shea came home drunk again. Janice and I also started noticing that Shea was smoking blunts. At first, we didn't say anything to Shea about his smoking habits, but after a while I told him to stop bringing his friends around our house to smoke with him in the backyard. As a result, Shea started staying over his friends' houses.

FROM TRAGEDY TO TRIUMPH

~~~~~~

"These things I have spoken unto you, that in me ye might have peace. In the world ye shall have tribulation: but be of good cheer; I have overcome the world."

John 16:33

Chapter 2

Our Story – The Day of Darkness

"The LORD is my shepherd; I shall not want. He maketh me to lie down in green pastures: he leadeth me beside the still waters. He restoreth my soul: he leadeth me in the paths of righteousness for his name's sake. Yea, though I walk through the valley of the shadow of death, I will fear no evil: for thou art with me; thy rod and thy staff they comfort me. Thou preparest a table before me in the presence of mine enemies: thou anointest my head with oil; my cup runneth over. Surely goodness and mercy shall follow me all the days of my life: and I will dwell in the house of the LORD forever."
Psalm 23:1-6

******

On July 17, 2012 (5:00am)

Shea came home. He walked over to the refrigerator, pulled his food out and put it in the microwave. He walked to his room, went back downstairs bypassing the microwave and went back into the refrigerator. When Shea realized his food was not in the refrigerator he came upstairs, woke me up out of sleep and startled my wife. Shea pushed me and said, "Come on man, why did you eat my food!" My dog Rusty heard the noise and went downstairs to hide under the table.

Shea and I both went down the stairs and I looked in the refrigerator for his food. I said to him, "I didn't eat your plate of food. All I ate was a bowl of Cheerios." Something told me to look in the microwave and when I did his food was there.

Shea balled up his fists as if he was going to hit me, and I saw the evil in his face. He started pushing me as I yelled at him to "Stop." My wife also had seen him pushing me and yelled "Stop Shea!" I told Shea he needed to stop disrespecting me or he had to get out my house. I sensed something was wrong, so I told Janice to call 9-1-1. My wife went into the bathroom and made the call and I went back up the stairs to our bedroom.

Shea followed me upstairs and as he yelled, "I am going to kill you!" When I heard him, I asked what he had meant? He then went into his room and came back with my zip lock bag. He put it on the chair, opened the bag and pulled out a thirty-eight-revolver gun. As I went to get it out of his hands he aggressively pushed me back. Shea then pulled the trigger and began shooting at me. I saw the bullet in slow motion as smoke emerged from the gun. At that moment, the Holy Spirit moved my body and the bullet ricocheted off my head. Shea shot the gun again and this time a bullet hit my chest. Then he shot me in my arm and again in my thumb on my right hand. At this moment, I had been shot four times. My wife ran out of the bathroom, and screamed, "Shea, Stop, you are killing him!" All I could hear were more shots as he turned around and shot at her two times.

My wife ran back in the bedroom, locked the door behind her and yelled at Shea to leave her alone. Shea followed her and tried to break the door down.

I wanted to help her, but I heard the Holy Spirit say, "Don't worry about her." I couldn't help it. All I wanted to do was help my wife, but the Holy Spirit was speaking to me. He told me that I was getting weak and that I needed to go hide in the hallway bathroom. I listened to His voice and made my way there. He said, "Crack the door and wait for Shea."

At this time, Shea went back downstairs to reload the gun. My wife ran downstairs behind him and asked him why he was behaving this way. He looked at her and didn't respond. My wife quickly ran out of the house. He reloaded the gun and came back upstairs to look for me. As soon as he walked past the bathroom, the Holy Spirit told me to get out of the house. Shea and I passed each other in the hallway, but it was as if God put a protective invisible shield around me so that Shea couldn't see me.

As I was leaving the house, I wondered why he didn't hear me. I ran out quickly and slammed the door closed. When Shea heard the door slam he looked out the window, saw me, and started shooting again. I reached a stop sign and tried to wave down a truck that was passing by, but they didn't stop. At this point I was bleeding from head to toe. I could feel my body getting weaker and weaker, but I knew I needed to get myself to a neighbor's house so that I could try and ring the doorbell. As I was running down the street my body was so weak that it shifted, and I fell into my neighbor's van that was parked in his driveway. I fell from there into the street and I laid there, my body covered in blood and my strength draining from me.

I thank God there were vehicles blocking Shea from seeing me. The police arrived, and I told them I was thirsty. I told the officer three times I was thirsty, but he replied he could not give me anything to drink as he called the ambulance over to me.

While waiting for the paramedics, I could feel my life departing from me. I could hear them yelling, "We are losing him." At that moment, I was caught in a tornado tunnel; I could feel myself drifting away. I heard an officer say, "Come back!" I also heard another officer say, "Get Down!" It was then that I felt my life return to me as I looked over and saw my wife standing there holding a phone in her hand. Seeing my wife alive in that moment gave me hope. I began to wonder what was going on. The SWAT Team demanded that my wife "DROP IT!" (They soon realized she was only holding a phone.) It was then that my wife heard one more gunshot and just knew that Shea had killed himself.

There were two ambulance vehicles at the scene (one for my wife and me; the other for Shea). The ambulance that we were in had to stop at the middle school in our neighborhood and medivac me to the hospital. I was losing consciousness and unable to identify my wife. When I arrived at the hospital, the medical team rolled me away. They cut my clothes off and put a respirator on me. They didn't realize I was having trouble breathing with the respirator on; every time it came off they would put it right back on. I believe it was the Holy Spirit that kept knocking the respirator off me, all five times. My jaw started locking up and they put a breathing tube down my throat. Then I passed out.

I was placed in a room and my wife had requested to see me. I could hear her voice as she reached out to touch me. When her hand touched me, my body started pulsating and the nurse had to come in and calm me down. When I awoke later my pastor and his wife were standing over me. I said to them, I forgive Shea with no idea of what had happened to him. My pastor let me call into the church one Sunday morning, to speak to the congregation on the loud speaker about my testimony and to thank everyone for all their prayers; they were felt. My brother and sisters and son all came to see me as well which really made me happy.

While in the hospital, I watched the news on TV and heard the news; Shea had killed himself. I wept for Shea, my son, as I continued to watch the news showing the SWAT Team surrounding our house. Three hours later, while watching the news again, the camera was shown in the window of my house looking for my son, Shea. The news stated that Shea was found lying on the bed with a gunshot wound to his head. The news also recorded our dog Rusty running out of the house to where my bloody body had lain. The police were amazed.

My decision to forgive Shea was the beginning of my body healing. The doctors had decided to send me home, but my brother told them that I was not ready. He told the doctor to look at my eyes and see that I was still weak. My blood pressure was dropping, and the doctors found out that I had blood clots. I thank God, my brother was at the hospital because it turned out I needed more blood, so I ended up staying in the hospital longer. My sister-in-law was a huge help and comfort to my wife Janice while I was in the hospital.

As I was in the process of healing, I was thankful for my co-workers from the Mover's Truck Leasing family being a support. They expressed their concerns for me and were willing to fill out my short-term disability forms. After seven days in the hospital, the doctors discharged me to go home. My sister's husband drove me to the hotel where my wife was staying since the tragic incident.

They placed me in the bed to rest since my body was still very weak and I was having shortness of breath. I kept having nightmares about the shooting and it took me about four weeks to gain my physical strength back. My wife and I lived at the hotel for about six months and from time-to-time, we would go back to visit our home. It was so hard to be there. My family, who went with us, would notice that I was always looking at the top window with a sense of nervousness. I was so overwhelmed with sadness and grief that I started seeing a Christian counselor. I had counseling sessions for about six months and was diagnosed with a 309.81 post-traumatic stress disorder.

Our family and friends' love and prayers kept my wife and I moving forward. People were so generous, blessing us with monetary gifts. They would remind us that God's grace was sufficient. We eventually began to prepare the house for our return. One day, my cousin's girlfriend, Janae was helping my wife place curtains on the windows.

When I came into the house, I looked up the stairs and tried to turn the lights on, but I had a flashback of the entire scene. It was Janae, who realized I was having the flashback. Soon after, my pastor and his wife came over to bless my house. He encouraged me to walk around the house with him and ask God to bless the inside of it. Four days later, we moved back in. The first night was rough for us; so much so that we both had to take Zolpidem Tartrate (sleeping pills) just to get any rest. We both wanted so badly to be able to sleep and keep our minds off the incident.

Eventually I ran out of pills and started taking Advil-PM. I remember one night taking three pills to numb myself from all the stress, worry and concern. The incident kept replaying in my mind. My heart started beating fast and as I laid down to sleep I could feel my heart rate gradually rising. I told my wife that I took too many pills and I was about to tell her to call 9-1-1 but I went outside instead to get some fresh air and calm myself down and then my heart stopped racing.

FROM TRAGEDY

TO

TRIUMPH

~~~~~~

"But thanks be to God, which giveth us the victory through our Lord Jesus Christ."

1 Corinthians 15:57

Chapter 3

Many Months After

"Forbearing one another, and forgiving one another, if any man has a quarrel against any: even as Christ forgave you, so also do ye."
Colossians 3:13

✶✶✶✶✶✶

Again, my wife and I thank God for Pastor Bobby Holmes, his wife, and the Deliverance Church of Christ. They were a great source of strength through our tragedy. Their spiritual guidance and support played a key role in our emotional and spiritual healing. My friends and neighbors were so loving toward us during this time.

"Greater love hath no man than this, that a man lay down his life for his friends." (John 15:13)

Every day was a struggle for us to keep living in the house where the tragedy occurred, but we took one day at a time. Eventually, I started going out and would see people. I was able to tell my story about the incident. As I shared with people, their hearts were touched. I started going back to my church at Deliverance Church of Christ.

Pastor Bobby allowed me to tell my testimony to the congregation and I thanked everyone for their prayers and support. I started back serving as an usher and singing with the music ministry which really helped in my healing process even though I had my moments of grief and sorrow. Getting back involved allowed me to not focus so much on the incident but rather lean into to Jesus as my comforter and healer.

My wife was still having a hard time. It was difficult for her to return to church and get back involved in ministry. She was still grieving the loss of our son, Shea. I would give her space because I knew she needed it and I didn't want to push her away from church.

Several months had passed when some friends of ours called and invited us to their church. The church was called New Hope Church of God. It took us about four weeks before we finally decided to attend with them.

My wife and I enjoyed attending the church. The pastors and church family were very friendly and made us feel welcome. On this Sunday, Pastor Jones was preaching a good word about God's love and we could feel the presence of God so strong that we decided to attend again. We began attending New Hope on a regular basis, but soon after my wife started staying home again. It was about a period of six months that my wife chose to stay home but I continued to attend. I knew she was still grieving. I had my moments of grief as well, but I kept attending the church and eventually my wife started going back with me. Soon after we decided to join the church and began attending New Members classes. I joined the usher ministry. As

I served as an usher, my left leg would ache from the injury but somehow, I pressed my way through.

I would be in so much pain on my job as well, but I would press my way to work every day just being thankful that I had the ability to still work. I was thankful that my boss would let me work every day and I knew that it was only by the grace of God that I was still here, alive and able to press my way through.

I tried to let my light shine around anyone I encountered, which can sometimes be a difficult task when you lose someone close to you. My faith in God and His grace is what carried me and continues to carry me through.

FROM TRAGEDY TO TRIUMPH

~~~~~~

"Wherefore take unto you the whole armour of God, that ye may be able to withstand in the evil day, and having done all, to stand."

Ephesians 6:13

Chapter 4

Relationship with My Son

"Children, obey your parents in the Lord: for this is right. Honour thy father and mother; which is the first commandment with promise; That it may be well with thee, and thou mayest live long on the earth. And, ye fathers, provoke not your children to wrath: but bring them up in the nurture and admonition of the Lord."
Ephesians 6:1-4

******

I had a good relationship with my son. Like every father-son relationship, we had our problems. I would teach him right from wrong. When Shea would get in trouble, I would talk to him about his behavior and how it would affect his life. There were times when Shea would go out with his friends and come home after drinking. I didn't like it and I would talk to him about the choices he was making and why those choices would not turn out for his good. He started getting better. I eventually helped Shea purchase a used car but then he started drinking again.

Shea was constantly getting in trouble. He was involved in a car accident because of his drinking and found himself in trouble with the police quite often. He was arrested and sent to a boy's village for a while. He was later sent to a camp called Old Dominion about two hours away from us. My wife and I would visit him, express to him how much we loved him and would pray for him daily.

Page left blank intentionally

FROM TRAGEDY

TO

TRIUMPH

~~~~~~

"For whatsoever is born of God overcometh the world: and this is the victory that overcometh the world, even our faith."

1 John 5:4

Chapter 5

You Never Know

My wife and I did not know that our son, Shea was depressed. We did notice that he was constantly sleeping during the day and going out at night. I remember asking Shea on several occasions, "Are you okay?" and he would always reply "I'm okay." My wife and I both decided to leave him alone. It wasn't until later we realized he was struggling with depression. Most people have no idea about the reality of the elaborate drug "K2," commonly known as Spice. It is an awful synthetic drug that resembles Marijuana and is traditionally smoked. Authentic K2, although a mirror drug, causes horrific side effects, ranging from hallucinations to suicide. When found in the hands of an adolescent only the worst is to be expected. Someone taking the drug K2 may be unresponsive or experience aggressive panic attacks. This drug can turn your everyday person into a zombie.

As a parent, you never know what is going through your children's minds or how they may feel on any given day. At times I would think back to that terrifying night. I would go in Shea's room and try to sit down but that night would always come back to me. It replayed over and over in my head and I would have to keep the lights on when I was in there. I would always wonder, "What would make Shea kill himself?"

Some nights, I would notice that I kept the light on in Shea's room. When I exit my room, I would see his room and the flashbacks would start all over again. I could not stop thinking about Shea killing himself. I would always pray and ask God to give me peace and the Holy Spirit would always remind me that Jesus saved us from ourselves. I know that if it had not been for the people praying for us, we would not have made it this far. Prayer definitely makes a difference. I continued to take one day at a time and trust the grace of God to carry me through.

I often pray for parents. I pray that the Lord will bless and guide them through the day. I pray for God's protection and love always. God's promises are true. He promises never to leave or forsake us. I pray that parents can cast their cares upon Jesus. He will always carry them through. Be in agreement with one another. Matthew 18:19 says, *"Again I say unto you, That if two of you shall agree on earth as touching anything that they shall ask, it shall be done for them of my Father which is in heaven."* When the road you are traveling seems difficult, at best, just remember I am here praying for you. My prayer is that God will give you rest.

Page left blank intentionally

FROM TRAGEDY

TO

TRIUMPH

~~~~~~

"And the LORD said unto Joshua, Fear them not: for I have delivered them into thine hand; there shall not a man of them stand before thee."

Joshua 10:8

Chapter 6

Our Lives Today

"The LORD is my light and my salvation; whom shall I fear? the LORD is the strength of my life; of whom shall I be afraid?"
Psalm 27:1

✶✶✶✶✶✶

I am currently employed at Mover's Truck Leasing and attending New Hope Church of God where I am an usher. My wife and I both enjoy it. The church congregation embraces us with Christian love. Sometimes I find myself feeling tired and overwhelmed, but it is the grace of God that gives me the strength to go on day to day. Whenever I think of what happened to my wife and I on July 17, 2012, it reminds me of how great God's grace is. It is God's grace that saved us both.

I believe that if we were not Christians, we would not be here on earth today. God has a mission on earth for us as Christians. God's desire is for us to lead people into the saving knowledge of Jesus Christ. I sincerely believe if God's hand was not working in our lives, we would not have made it through that night or all the nights that have followed. When our son Shea was shooting at us, the Holy Spirit was speaking to us, telling us how to hide in the house. God's divine intervention allowed us to make it out of that tragic incident. If we would have allowed our fear to override the voice of God, we would not have gotten out of the house alive that night. We yielded to the voice of the Holy Spirit (God's voice) we yielded to the voice of the Holy Spirit (God's voice, instead of giving into fear. His voice was smoother than water. God really speaks to us; it's up to us to listen and obey. Much too often we become so busy with our lives that we do not make time for God until something happens. Learn to take time, even with everything going on around you to just be still. Meditate on God's goodness and receive from Him.

On July 17, 2012, when our son came home that night and shot me several times, we could not believe in our hearts that he was trying to kill us. It changed our lives forever. We have watched television shows where children had killed their parents, but never in all our lives did we think we would go through something like it. It was that experience that caused us to look at life differently. We live life to the fullest now. Don't take things for granted; life is precious, and you never know when your last breath will be. Love people the way you want to be loved and always be thankful for the life God has given you.

I am a little better today. I go to work every day, but the incident still crosses my mind from time-to-time. My wife, Janice, is still having a difficult time. She is still grieving and missing Shea, but she is getting better one day at a time.

No one may know what you have been through or what you are feeling after experiencing such a trauma, but God's grace is what carries you forth. Sometimes my wife takes a break from church and I try to allow her the time to grieve. When she returns to church, she is so happy being surrounded by her church family. I can't thank God enough for those that are constantly covering our family in prayer.

On a daily basis, we are seeking spiritual guidance to help us function. We try to let go and let God take full control of our lives. We kneel and pray more; we read the Bible daily and try to live our lives in a way that draws people to the light of Jesus. We pray that people will see Christ in our lives and find joy after encountering us. God encouraged my wife and I through His word (the Bible) while we were going through the darkest season of our lives. He gave us both a reason to have joy, even in our darkest moment. We still had our rough days from time to time, but we continued to read God's word. In doing so we received daily encouragement and prayers to help us through. Our church family's prayers for us meant the world to us. They prayed that God would use our pain to glorify His name, that He would lift us up and deliver us from our heartache.

When we tell our story and people see how happy we are, they are amazed. We tell them that it is because of God's love and grace that we are here. We know people are watching our lives when we say that we are Christians. We want to represent Christ well. When you love God and put God first in every aspect of your life, then you will be satisfied. God's love will flow out of your life and onto those around you. It is then that you will feel true happiness in your life. When you go on your job people will see that you are happy. They may begin asking you "why are you so happy?" Then, you can tell them about Jesus Christ, that He died on the cross for us, so we may have life and have it more abundantly. We will always remember God's hand over our lives,

Psalm 91:1-6, says it best:

> *"He that dwelleth in the secret place of the most high shall abide under the shadow of the almighty. I will say of the Lord, He is my refuge and my fortress; my God in Him will trust. Surely, He shall deliver thee from the snare of the fowler, and from the noisome pestilence. He shall cover thee with his feathers, and under His wings shalt thou trust; his truth shall be thy shield and buckler. Thou shalt not be afraid for the terror by night; nor for the arrow that flieth by day; Nor for the pestilence that walketh in darkness; nor for the destruction that wasteth at noonday."*

Page left blank intentionally

FROM TRAGEDY

TO

TRIUMPH

~~~~~~

And thou shalt teach them diligently unto thy children, and shalt talk of them when thou sittest in thine house, and when thou walkest by the way, and when thou liest down, and when thou risest up.

Deuteronomy 6:7

Message to the Parents

If I there was anything, I could get out of this tragic incident for parents it would be that we need to pay more attention to our children. They are struggling daily with problems they may be unwilling to share with us. We as parents need to be more aware of the warning signs and the unusual behaviors. When you notice your children lying around not wanting to do anything, don't take it lightly or brush it off like nothing is wrong. Your child may be struggling with depression. It is up to us as parents to recognize these warning signs and do something about it.

Your children may not immediately tell you what is on their minds, but please do not wait until after they have killed themselves to find out the problem. Take appropriate steps before it's too late. If they won't talk to you, find someone they are comfortable talking with, so they can get the help they need. We later found out, after Shea's death, that he was experimenting with a drug called K2. This drug causes hallucination and agitation.

My wife and I wished we could have helped Shea. We did see some signs of depression, but we over looked it; we ignored it. I would ask him how he was doing, his response was always, "I'm okay!", but I could see something was wrong. Shea would sleep all day and at night he would come home drunk. In the morning, we knew not to bother him because he would be angry. Parents, bother your children and involve yourself in their problems. For my wife and I it's too late to find out that Shea was on this drug and do something. This drug, K2 can easily be purchased over-the-counter in stores, it broke our hearts and he learned about this drug from his so-called friends. Parents pay attention to who your children are hanging around and choosing to befriend. Sometimes knowing the people that are around your children can identify the things they are involving themselves in. Don't be afraid to ask questions, it could be a matter of life or death.

LETTER OF COMMENDATION

Rex W. Coffey, Chief Sheriff
Charles County Sheriff's Office
3680 Leonardtown Rd,
Waldorf, Maryland 20602

Dear Chief Coffey:

We are sending this letter to acknowledge the outstanding service performed by officers in your department and to express our sincere gratitude.

On Tuesday, July 17, 2012, my wife and I were shot multiple times by our son who, in the end, took his own life. It was somewhere between 5:00 and 5:30 am that morning when the police arrived on the scene. **PFC Stephen Duley – Badge #494**, was the first office there who assisted me. I remember him coming over, holding my hand and he just kept talking to me (I believe he was trying to keep me conscious), and that helped me to stay calm. He cared enough to "want to" stay right there with me and try to help me anyway he could. It really touched me even more when he later told me that I had died on the scene.

I am so thankful to Officer Duley for being there at the right time to administer his help. And, with his help, God spared my life. I feel he went above and beyond his call of duty that morning because he showed it just wasn't a job to him but an opportunity to show how important it is to save a life. So, from the bottom of our hearts, my wife and I want to tell him, "Thank you so, so much for all he did to help us through that time of turmoil and tragedy. We will never forget his act of kindness and servitude toward us." For this we feel he should be commended!

Also, there were several other officers on duty who we would like to thank for their help: Sgt. Kevin Keetan – Badge #265; PFC Herbert – Badge #399; PFC Alvarez – Badge #258; COL Leukhardt – Badge #257; and POL Clark – Badge #556. These officers played an active part in helping us through the events of that morning, as well. You should be very proud to have them as a part of your team.

We want you to always remember that we do appreciate all that you do to serve our county and keep us safe. Again, we say, THANK YOU!

With Sincere Gratitude,

Mr. & Mrs. Jeffrey Wills

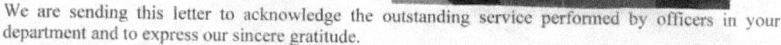

Letter of Commendation

www.ingramcontent.com/pod-product-compliance
Lightning Source LLC
Chambersburg PA
CBHW071549080526
44588CB00011B/1837